Female FOODIES

Debbi Fields

Mrs. Fields Founder

Rebecca Felix

Checkerboard
Library

An Imprint of Abdo Publishing
abdopublishing.com

abdopublishing.com

Published by Abdo Publishing, a division of ABDO, PO Box 398166, Minneapolis, Minnesota 55439. Copyright © 2018 by Abdo Consulting Group, Inc. International copyrights reserved in all countries. No part of this book may be reproduced in any form without written permission from the publisher. Checkerboard Library™ is a trademark and logo of Abdo Publishing.

Printed in the United States of America, North Mankato, Minnesota
102017
012018

THIS BOOK CONTAINS
RECYCLED MATERIALS

Design: Sarah DeYoung, Mighty Media, Inc.
Production: Mighty Media, Inc.
Editor: Liz Salzmann
Cover Photographs: AP Images; Mighty Media, Inc.
Interior Photographs: AP Images, p. 17; Ashley Hylbert Photography, p. 23; iStockphoto, pp., 5, 29 (bottom); Ron Riesterer Photography, pp. 9, 28 (top); Shutterstock, pp. 13, 19, 21, 25, 28 (bottom); Yearbook Library, pp. 7, 11, 15, 29 (top)
Background Pattern: Shutterstock, cover, pp. 3, 5, 7, 9, 11, 13, 15, 17, 19, 21, 23, 25, 31

Publisher's Cataloging-in-Publication Data
Names: Felix, Rebecca, author.
Title: Debbi Fields: Mrs. Fields founder / by Rebecca Felix.
Other titles: Mrs. Fields founder
Description: Minneapolis, Minnesota : Abdo Publishing, 2018. | Series: Female foodies |
    Includes online resources and index.
Identifiers: LCCN 2017944041 | ISBN 9781532112683 (lib.bdg.) | ISBN 9781532150401 (ebook)
Subjects: LCSH: Fields, Debra, 1956-.--Juvenile literature. | Businesswomen--United States--Biography--
    Juvenile literature. | Cookie industry--Juvenile literature. | Entrepreneurship--Juvenile literature.
Classification: DDC 338.76647 [B]--dc23
LC record available at https://lccn.loc.gov/2017944041

Contents

Chapter 1

Cookie Entrepreneur

It's Sunday and you're meeting friends at the mall **arcade**. You walk through the double doors and toward the sounds of video games. Then another sense takes over. The scent of fresh-baked cookies is in the air. You follow your nose and aren't surprised to see a Mrs. Fields sign. You know the cookies there will indeed be freshly baked. And each warm cookie will be soft, chewy, and super tasty!

Mrs. Fields is one of the best-known names in cookies. It is also a name that belongs to a real person! Debbi Fields is the baking **entrepreneur** behind these famous sweet treats. Fields began her cookie empire in California when she was just 20 years old. Today, there are more than 700 Mrs. Fields locations in ten countries!

Fields is the namesake, founder, and public face behind Mrs. Fields. Each cookie in these stores is made exactly to Fields's **specifications**. This hands-on boss and baker discovered her cookie making skills at a young age. She has been perfecting them ever since.

Many people have tried to recreate Mrs. Fields cookies at home, but the original is hard to beat!

Chapter 2

California Childhood

Debra Jane Sivyer was born on September 18, 1956, in Oakland, California. She went by Debbi. Debbi had four older sisters, Linda, Mary, Marlene, and Cathy. The Sivyer sisters' father was a **welder**. Their mother took care of the household and children.

Debbi's family did not have a lot of money. But Debbi says her mother "could make a dollar stretch forever." Debbi's parents taught their daughters that there was no sense in dreaming or wishing for something. Instead, they believed that you could get what you wanted by working hard.

The Sivyers also taught Debbi that family and doing what makes you happy were more important than money. Learning how to fail was another important family lesson. Debbi credits learning these lessons for her future success in the cookie business.

Food Bite

In addition to baking, Debbi loved to water ski and snow ski. She learned to water ski when she was five years old!

During Debbi's childhood, the kitchen was the family's main gathering place.

Debbi began baking at age 13 in her parents' kitchen. There, she used what was on hand to make chocolate chip cookies. This included imitation chocolate chips, imitation vanilla flavoring, and margarine instead of butter. These ingredients cost less than pure ingredients. But at the time, Debbi felt the cookies she made with them were top quality!

Chapter 3

Cookies and Baseball

As Debbi grew skilled at baking, she often shared her treats with friends and family. Some family members began calling her "the cookie kid." Debbi loved the positive reaction people had to her cookies.

Debbi also took cookies to share with people at her first job. When she was 13, Debbi became a ball girl for the Major League Baseball team the Oakland A's. Her duty was to catch stray baseballs and return them to an umpire or the **dugout**.

During games, Debbi passed out her cookies between **innings**. The players and ballpark staff thought they tasted wonderful. The response to Debbi's cookies made her realize they might be something special. She knew she could make a tasty cookie with lower-priced, imitation ingredients. But now that she had her own money to spend, she wanted to see if purer ingredients would improve her cookies.

Debbi used money she earned from the Oakland A's to buy quality chocolate, real butter, and real vanilla. She was

Debbi was an Oakland A's ball girl when the team won its first World Series championship in 1972.

shocked by the difference! The quality ingredients made a much better cookie. Debbi decided she would only use the best ingredients in her baked goods.

Chapter 4
Work Ethic

Baking and her role as a ball girl taught Debbi that she liked to bring other people joy. It also taught her that everyone wants to feel important. This became a key ingredient in her future success.

Other jobs Debbi had as a teen also taught her valuable lessons. She worked at a department store called Mervyn's for a time. There, Debbi learned how important it was to make customers happy. She became skilled at customer service.

Then Debbi got a job at a local aquarium called Marine World. Debbi performed in water-skiing shows. Later, Debbi was promoted to swimming with the dolphins during Marine World shows. She held their fins as they pulled her around a pool.

The values Debbi developed at her jobs became the foundation for her future career. But before she began her career, Debbi wanted adventure. She graduated from high school in 1974. Then, she moved to the Lake Tahoe area to try and make it on her own.

Debbi was voted Homecoming Queen during her senior year of high school.

Chapter 5

New Adventures

Sivyer arrived in Lake Tahoe full of energy and hope. She found an apartment and got a job as a nanny. She cared for five children and cleaned their family home. When Sivyer wasn't working, she was often skiing, which had become a favorite pastime.

However, living in Lake Tahoe turned out to be a short adventure. Within a few months, Sivyer decided to move back home to Oakland. There, she worked in **retail** stores and lived with her parents. She used the money she earned to go on ski trips. During a ski trip to Colorado, she met Randy Fields in an airport in Denver.

Randy was an **economist** who sometimes visited Oakland for work. He was 28, ten years older than Sivyer. Randy spoke with Sivyer as they waited for their separate flights. He asked for her telephone number and called

Food Bite

Sivyer drove herself to Lake Tahoe and back in her orange Volkswagen Beetle.

The Lake Tahoe area is popular for skiing, snowboarding, hiking, and more!

the next day. Sivyer and Randy began dating, seeing one another when Randy was in town on business.

Meanwhile, Sivyer took a few classes at a community college. But her college career was short-lived. Sivyer married Randy on September 21, 1976, and took his last name. The couple got an apartment in Menlo Park, California. Fields returned to college for a short time, but did not finish her studies. Instead, she became a housewife.

Chapter 6

From Insult to Idea

At first, Fields was happy to be a housewife. She enjoyed taking care of her new home and baking for her husband. The Fieldses often attended dinner parties with Randy's **colleagues**. Fields usually brought a batch of fresh-baked cookies. Everyone loved Fields's treats! Their reactions made her feel important.

But other aspects of these dinner parties made Fields feel just the opposite. Many of Randy's colleagues looked down on her because she didn't have a career. During one dinner party, a man named Sandy Lewis asked Fields about her life goals. Fields told him she was still getting "orientated." Hearing this, Lewis told her the word she should have used was "oriented." Lewis told Fields to learn proper English.

Fields was hurt and embarrassed. But the incident affected her another way too. She decided she never again wanted to feel badly about herself. She wanted to do something important with her life. In that moment, Fields turned a dinner-party insult into the idea for Mrs. Fields.

Fields started her business to prove herself to others. But she also discovered her own worth!

Chapter 7

Chocolate Chippery

Fields's plan was to open a bakery specializing in chocolate chip cookies. A bakery selling only cookies would be the first of its kind. And everyone she talked to about it thought it was a bad idea. Even Randy was uncertain. He found studies that said US buyers liked crispy cookies. But the ones Fields made were soft and slightly chewy.

Still, Fields believed her cookies would sell. She had spent years seeing people's positive reactions to them. Finally, Fields got a loan covering part of the cost to open a shop. Randy gave her the rest of the money needed. She rented a small shop in Palo Alto and got to work. At just 20 years old, Fields was officially a business owner.

Fields spent three weeks baking and perfecting her recipe. Mrs. Fields' Chocolate Chippery opened in August 1977. The night before, Randy had jokingly bet her that she

Food Bite

Fields's **slogan** was, "Some people take flour and add chocolate chips. We take chocolate chips and add flour."

Fields once said, "I knew I loved making cookies and every time I did, I made people happy. That was my business plan."

wouldn't make $50 the first day. Fields was charging 25 cents per cookie, so she would need to sell 200 cookies to win the bet. By noon, she hadn't sold even one.

Chapter 8

Sweet Success

Fields was upset about the lack of sales. She felt her potential customers were missing out on something great. So, she decided to give her cookies away if people weren't going to buy them. Fields asked a friend to watch the store. Then she loaded a tray with cookies and hit the streets. One by one, Fields gave the entire tray of cookies to passersby.

Empty tray in hand, Fields returned to the shop to bake more cookies. Soon, some of the people who had tried her cookies on the street came to the store to buy more! Fields made $50 in sales that day, winning her bet with Randy.

Fields's shop soon earned regular customers. When it had been open for only a few months, one customer changed Fields's life and the future of the store. Warren Simmons was building a shopping mall in San Francisco, California. He wanted there to be

Food Bite

Fields says, "If you chase money, you'll never catch it." She believes you should love what you do, not the money you make doing it.

Pier 39 is a mall
built on a pier.
It features shops,
restaurants, an
arcade, and
an aquarium.

a Mrs. Fields' Chocolate Chippery in the new mall. Simmons
thought Fields's cookies could become a big business.

Fields was flattered by the offer, but turned Simmons
down. She hadn't gone into the cookie business to make
money. She just wanted to make something people would
enjoy. And it gave her a purpose in life. Fields felt that was
enough.

Chapter 9

Expansion

Mrs. Fields' Chocolate Chippery stayed busy. Soon after the shop's one-year **anniversary**, Simmons reached out to Fields again. The Pier 39 mall was now open in San Francisco. He was holding a spot for a cookie shop in case Fields changed her mind.

This time, Fields accepted. Her second cookie shop opened in the Pier 39 mall in 1979. It proved to be just as successful as the first. The lines of cookie customers sometimes blocked the doorways of other stores! Customer service was important to Fields. She found the better she treated her customers, the more cookies they bought.

Fields was also committed to only selling perfect cookies. Once, Fields entered one of her shops and saw that the cookies were too brown. They were also the wrong size. So, Fields threw them all away!

Fields trained her workers to test each cookie. To do this, an employee picks up a cookie with a tissue. Then, he or she presses the bottom of the cookie. If the cookie is soft, it can be sold. If not, the employee discards the cookie.

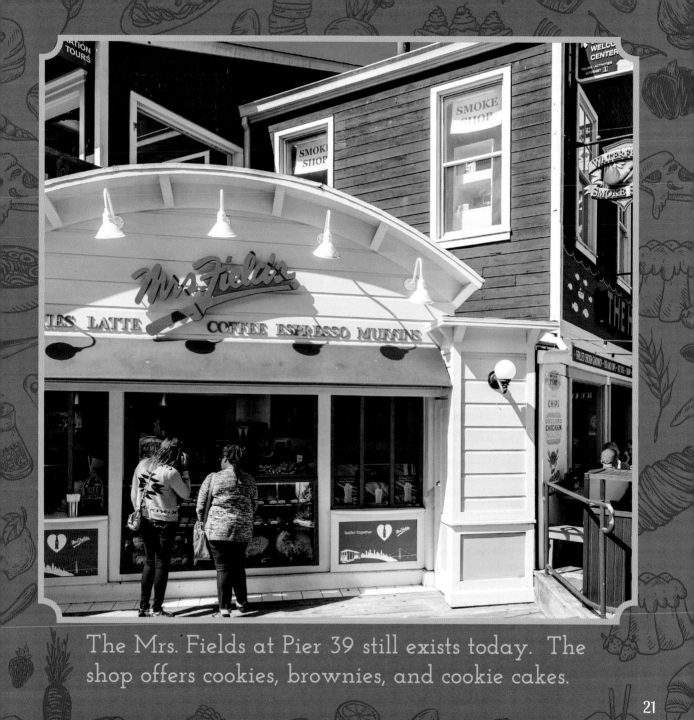

The Mrs. Fields at Pier 39 still exists today. The shop offers cookies, brownies, and cookie cakes.

Chapter 10

Family and Business

The Mrs. Fields' Chocolate Chippery locations were very successful. And they started selling more than just chocolate chip cookies. Fields made other kinds of cookies, such as oatmeal raisin and peanut butter. She soon shortened the company name to Mrs. Fields.

As company sales grew, Fields and Randy's family also expanded. In 1979, the couple welcomed a daughter, Jessica. Jessica was just one month old when she traveled with her parents to Hawaii. They later opened the third Mrs. Fields location there.

In 1981, Fields had her second daughter, Jenessa. The company continued to grow rapidly. By 1982, they decided to make the business international. Mrs. Fields stores opened in Japan, Hong Kong, and Australia in the following years.

Also in 1982, the Fields family moved to Utah. There, Fields

Food Bite

Fields's daughters Jessica, Jenessa, and Jennifer also love baking. Ashley and McKenzie like to decorate desserts.

In 1987, Fields released her first book, *One Smart Cookie: How a Housewife's Chocolate Chip Recipe Turned into a Multimillion-Dollar Business.*

established the Mrs. Fields, Inc., company headquarters in Park City. Then, between 1984 and 1991, Fields had three more daughters. They were Jennifer, Ashley, and McKenzie.

During this time, Fields continued expanding her product line. Mrs. Fields stores now sold 14 types of cookies. These included Pecan Whites, Peanut Butter Dreams, Raisin Spice, and more. Fields also made and sold brownies, ice cream, candy, and muffins.

Chapter 11

Global Growth

Mrs. Fields, Inc., continued to expand. By the late 1980s, there were more than 500 locations! As stores spread across the nation and then world, Fields kept her commitment to quality. She prepackaged her quality ingredients and sent them to each store. At the stores, employees baked the treats to her standards. This made sure that customers at every Mrs. Fields shop received the same quality, chewy cookies.

But customers' tastes did vary by location. Certain types of cookies were more popular in certain locations. For example, macadamia nut cookies were a best seller in Mrs. Fields shops in Hawaii. Customers in Utah preferred the milk chocolate chip cookie. East Coast customers liked the cookies with dark chocolate chips.

Many recipes and hundreds of stores were a lot to keep track of. In 1989, Randy computerized Mrs. Fields. Each store used a **software** program to kept track of **inventory**, sales, and more. Around this time, Mrs. Fields, Inc., also began selling frozen cookie dough in US **supermarkets**.

Fields's top priority was maintaining the best quality products in each location.

Chapter 12
New Roles

The 1990s brought great change for Fields. In 1990, she **franchised** her company. Hotel giant Marriott Corporation opened 60 Mrs. Fields locations. Three years later, Fields sold most of the company to private investors. She continued to act as company spokesperson.

As her wealth and fame grew, Fields gave back to the community. She supported an organization that focused on research to cure **cystic fibrosis**. Fields also supported several education **boards**.

In 1997, Fields and Randy divorced. Fields married businessman Michael Rose the next year. Today, Fields lives in Memphis, Tennessee, with her husband. She travels the country sharing her story and knowledge about success in business.

Famous Brands International bought Mrs. Fields, Inc., in the 2000s. Even under new owners, Fields's vision of pleasing customers and using pure ingredients remains. And every chewy cookie and sweet treat is made to perfection, just as Fields would expect!

Debbi Fields

By the Numbers

1/2

thickness in inches (1.25 cm) of what Debbi says is a "perfect Mrs. Fields cookie"

3

width in inches (7.6 cm) of what Debbi says is a "perfect Mrs. Fields cookie"

14

number of Mrs. Fields locations in 1981

300

distance in feet (91 m) from which the scent of Mrs. Fields brownies being baked can be smelled

400

approximate number of US and international Mrs. Fields locations today

57,000

number of Nibblers bite-sized cookies the Mrs. Fields gift manufacturing facility can bake per hour

2,000,000

weight in pounds (907,185 kg) of cookie dough Mrs. Fields locations used in 2010

Timeline

1956

Debra Jane
Sivyer is born
on September
18 in Oakland,
California.

1970

Debbi gets a job as a ball
girl for the Oakland A's
baseball team.

1977

Fields opens the first
Mrs. Fields' Chocolate
Chippery in August.

1979

Fields opens her second
store in the Pier 39 mall
in San Francisco.

1997

Fields and Randy
get divorced.

28

1974
Debbie graduates from high school. She moves to the Lake Tahoe area.

1976
Sivyer marries Randy Fields and takes his last name.

1982
The Fields family moves to Utah and establishes the Mrs. Fields, Inc., headquarters there.

1998
Fields marries Michael Rose.

2000s
Famous Brands International buys Mrs. Fields, Inc.

Glossary

anniversary – the date of a special event that is often celebrated each year.

arcade – a place with electronic games that are operated by coins or tokens.

board – a group of people who manage, direct, or investigate.

colleague – someone you work with or who does the same kind of work as you.

cystic fibrosis – a disease that usually appears in young children and that makes it hard to breathe and to digest food.

dugout – the seating area for baseball team members who are not currently on the playing field.

economist – an expert in economics. Economics is the study of the way a nation produces and uses goods, services, and natural resources.

entrepreneur – one who organizes, manages, and accepts the risks of a business or an enterprise.

franchise – to grant someone the right to sell a company's goods or services in a particular place.

inning – a division of a baseball game that consists of a turn at bat for each team.

inventory – the quantity of goods or materials on hand.

retail – of or having to do with the sale of goods directly to customers.

slogan – a word or a phrase used to express a position, a stand, or a goal.

software – the written programs used to operate a computer.

specification – an instruction that says exactly how to do or make something.

supermarket – a large store that sells foods and household items.

welder – someone whose job is to join metal parts using heat.

Online Resources

Booklinks
NONFICTION
NETWORK
FREE! ONLINE NONFICTION RESOURCES

To learn more about Debbi Fields, visit **abdobooklinks.com**. These links are routinely monitored and updated to provide the most current information available.

Index